# THE ART OF MONEY MANAGEMENT

# THE ART OF MONEY MANAGEMENT

◆

## FOR A SIMPLE LIFE

*Janice Aldrow, B.S.*

# THE ART OF MONEY MANAGEMENT
## FOR A SIMPLE LIFE

*iUniverse books may be ordered through booksellers or by contacting:*

*iUniverse*
*1663 Liberty Drive*
*Bloomington, IN 47403*
*www.iuniverse.com*
*1-800-Authors (1-800-288-4677)*

*Because of the dynamic nature of the Internet, any web addresses or links contained in this book may have changed since publication and may no longer be valid. The views expressed in this work are solely those of the author and do not necessarily reflect the views of the publisher, and the publisher hereby disclaims any responsibility for them.*

*Any people depicted in stock imagery provided by Thinkstock are models, and such images are being used for illustrative purposes only. Certain stock imagery © Thinkstock.*

*ISBN: 978-0-5953-5800-7 (sc)*
*ISBN: 978-0-5958-0269-2 (e)*

*Print information available on the last page.*

*iUniverse rev. date: 08/12/20215*

# *Contents*

# *INTRODUCTION*

Always remember, and please never forget that money is merely a vehicle of exchange that we use to obtain the goods and services that we need to maintain a lifestyle that brings us some sense of satisfaction. The amount of money we have in our possession does not determine our character or intelligence, and it cannot bring us peace or joy. However, the proper management of money that includes a savings plan and pattern for debt management makes it possible to save for a vacation and purchase those things that provide physical security, resulting in peace and joy concerning the material aspects of our lives. The ideas and fundamental principles presented in this workbook are really truths that will not only help to manage finances, but other aspects of life as well. Shopping for the wisest purchase makes it clear that there is ALWAYS a choice to be made, no matter what the situation may be, and we will explore that idea with the Rational Decision Model. Keeping in touch with creditors will help develop problem-solving skills that will apply to any situation-not just with money.

I sincerely hope that you have begun using this workbook before you have had to deal with any financial crisis in your life. But, if you are in debt and need some help sorting things out, here are a few tips that will help. First, communication with your creditors will make all the difference in the world. They really are on your side. You will gain your creditors' respect and they will be much more cooperative when you let them know when an emergency has arisen, than if you did not communicate at all. Work out a new budget and call them to let them know how much you can afford to pay that month.

Place your credit cards and any other interest bearing loans at the top of your list of priorities. We will discuss credit card interest charges later on in the workbook, but you will get ahead faster in paying off the debt if you always make sure to pay more than the minimum amount charged, since most of that charge is interest and very little goes toward the principle, as the amount of the charges increase.

Check out your local branch of Consumer Credit Counseling Services if you are in debt over your head and need serious help. Individuals must qualify for this program, but the finance counselors will help you get back on track, and you will be able to use the principles in this workbook during your recovery period.

I was raised by a single mother and have had some unique experiences, not only as her only child, but with the life I experienced practicing some of the principles I learned as a child, in my adult years. I have included some short stories about the experiences surrounding my brief marriage, life as a single parent, and raising my two children who truly are my gifts from God. I hope my stories will enhance your understanding of choices, prioritizing, and the value of living with delayed gratification.

My children are grown now and both live independently, using the principles I have written in this book as well as the workbook itself. I only hope that the book will also enable you, dear reader, to establish a pattern of organization that my children and I enjoy.

This weekend l decided that, with Thanksgiving over, it was the perfect time to clean out the closets that stored all the Christmas presents I have collected throughout the year and take inventory of what I had, so I would know what else I needed to purchase to make the holiday complete. How much is enough? How does one find the balance between giving gifts to express love, sentiment, and joy, and the amount of resources (time, money, energy) available to feel satisfied with the number of presents shared?

The lifetime I have just completed had no room for that question. Raising my children alone answered that question before it even came to mind. It simplified my life tremendously in many ways. I knew exactly how much time, energy, and money I had to spend. The gifts that were given came from the heart, because since there was almost no money, the resources came in the shape of time that I made happen, and energy that was used to create something out of nothing. Those were tough years, but now in retrospect, I can cherish the lessons l learned about developing coping strategies, and about myself.

I will never forget the Christmas l did not get paid until Christmas Eve, and I did not have the resources to shop before payday, if I also wanted to pay the bills. I cashed my paycheck after work, took the kids over to my mother's house, and went to one of the local discount stores staying open until Midnight on Christmas Eve to do all of my shopping at 75% off all the Christmas merchandise. I ran home, wrapped the presents, placed them under the tree, and went back to Mom's to pick up my sleeping children. The timing was perfect, except for the fact that I didn't get much sleep that night. I gave Mom one more opportunity to feel needed and to enjoy her grandchildren, and I had a real sense of accomplishment at having provided for my family. Although I would never have chosen to provide Christmas that way, any more than I chose to raise my children without any support from their earthly father, I learned that even with all of the "things" I thought were lacking in my life, I was able to share the most important element of Christmas with my family, that being the love that God created us for, and the joy of sharing that love with the people God placed in my life. I consider myself blessed that I had the opportunity to learn that lesson, even though it meant giving up everything else in order to truly grasp how vital His love is to my life.

Well, maybe I'll get the kids one more present and call it good. After all, it is so fun to see the looks on their faces when they see that I didn't forget something they mentioned last summer.

This money management workbook is not just about money. The manner in which we spend our money, however, reflects our values, priorities, and our attitude about the role we play in relationship with our community. In this day and age, it may seem as though we have no time to share our lives with family or friends. Perhaps we do not even acknowledge that we are members of a community, since there seems to be no time at all after we do all of those things we feel we are supposed to do in order to maintain body and soul for ourselves, and our children. How strange it will seem, then, to share with the neighbor next door, after the children are grown and have left the nest, and hear that you were both feeling the same way, but never understood that you both were making the same choice without even realizing that you were making a choice.

Even as a clerical worker for an insurance company in Buffalo, New York, which provided enough money for a Christmas Club Account at my bank, I always enjoyed sharing the gifts I made with my hands above anything I could purchase in a store. I can see that following my heart in this area pulled me through those trying times, and even gave my family joy at overcoming the trials we were fortunate to experience. I believe that I was fortunate to experience those trials because those trials showed me how much I could believe in my own abilities to create, and it strengthened my faith and trust in God, who gave me everything I needed to overcome those insurmountable mountains that I would have to climb.

Think about your values and priorities as you read this book, and when you have decided what is most important to you at this stage of your life, I believe you will experience a sense of joy and satisfaction in finding a direction for your energy.

# *JANUARY*

## <u>INSTRUCTIONS FOR USING THIS WORKBOOK</u>

First of all, read through the entire workbook—it's not that long. I have included a couple of projects that will take a little time such as shopping for insurance and financial institutions for banking, that you can be prepared to do at your convenience. I would like to interject a word of encouragement at this point. Reading all of this information may be overwhelming at first, and if it does, just read the parts of the book that you feel need immediate attention, then read the rest more carefully in the not too distant future. Managing your finances is a discipline that may not be comfortable at this point in time. The most important facets will be different for everyone, but nevertheless, management is vitally important. Unpleasant surprises occur most often when we try to turn our backs on uncomfortable issues, but when we can see problems arising, especially in debt management, we may be able to plan ahead to manage those changes in our lives that forces a change in our priorities.

I originally designed this book as a financial "closet" that holds a Cash Flow Statement for each month as well as a Checking Account Balance sheet for monthly use. If you wish to create a hands-on folder that will hold all of your bills and receipts, plus any other important financial documents such as your tax return paperwork, you will need a three-ring binder and twelve double-sided folders, one for each month. The Cash Flow Statement I have included for each month needs to be completed as each bill and each paycheck comes into your possession. Record each paycheck under <u>Assets</u>, since any money that is available to use in order to maintain your lifestyle is an Asset. This also includes gifts, tips, and any other source of income. Then, store the pay stub or any other type of receipt that is written proof of that income in the back of the monthly folder to keep for your records. You will want to keep these documents for ten years for tax purposes.

Each debt on which payments are made is called a <u>Liability.</u> This includes the payment that you make to yourself each month that is listed as Savings. The savings you accrue will become an Asset when you are ready to spend it on the item you wish to purchase. Each time you receive a bill from a creditor, that is a company or individual to whom you are indebted, record the amount of the debt on the Liabilities side of your Cash Flow Statement. Each time you send a payment to a creditor, store the receipt in the pocket on the back of each monthly folder. Keep these receipts for ten years also. By recording and storing this information, you are creating a written record of spending habits that you will be able to study and learn from when the need arises, especially when your income changes. I will outline three methods that can be used to pay creditors and to purchase those items that maintain your lifestyle—The envelope method using cash and money orders, checking accounts, and credit cards. The first and simplest transaction, can be completed by using cash. Yes, cash is still around! and people receiving cash will never ask you for identification. You will always know how much of it you have spent, and, hence, how much you have left to spend!! Perfect! Be careful though, and make sure you ALWAYS receive a receipt before you consider the transaction complete. I will show you an envelope method of budgeting using cash and money orders that satisfies the need to use a hands-on method of spending your money.

When payments need to be mailed, cash is never recommended as a method of payment since it is easily lost or stolen and there is no receipt to prove that a payment has been made. Therefore, I highly recommend using money orders when necessary to manage your payments. Money orders are just like cash in the sense that one knows how much money is being spent and how much is left to spend because money orders can only be purchased with cash or a Debit card that withdraws money directly out of your checking account. Plus, you have the safety of a receipt and insurance that will cover the amount of the money order in case it is lost or stolen.

Cash and money orders are very tangible forms of managing one's finances, and is well suited for those people who just find it too complicated or abstract to sit down and play with numbers that represent the money they are working with on a daily basis. For those people who enjoy balancing a checkbook, playing with numbers, remembering the rules and never forgetting bank charges, I have information on checking accounts and the increasingly popular debit and credit cards later on in the book.

MONTH                              YEAR

INCOME (Assets)
Wages
Tips
Other Sources

++++++++++++++

FINANCIAL RESPONSIBILITIES (Liabilities)

Savings
Rent/House Payment                              Telephone
Heat                              Electricity
Food                              Transportation
Insurance                              Credit Card(s)
Miscellaneous

++++++++++++++++++++++++++++++++

Checks Outstanding not charged to Checking
  Account

No._____$_____                    <u>Line 1</u>

                                               Bank balance shown on this statement
_____                      $_____
                                               <u>Line 2</u>
_____              ADD new deposits
                                                       $_____
_____

                                               <u>Line 3</u>
_____              Deposits not credited in this statement
                                                       $_____
_____                      $_____
                                                       $_____
_____                      $_____
                                                       $_____

Total_____$_____                   <u>Line 4</u>
                                               TOTAL           $_____

                                               <u>Line 5</u>
                                               SUBTRACT outstanding checks
                                                       $_____

                                               BALANCE         $_____

                                               Should agree with your checkbook
                                               balance

# FEBRUARY

## THE ENVELOPE METHOD

The envelope method of budgeting consists of creating an envelope for each living expense you have to keep your household running smoothly. Those expenses will include Savings, Rent, Telephone, Heat, Electricity, Groceries, Transportation, Insurance, Entertainment, and Miscellaneous Expenses such as cosmetics, cleaning supplies, and the like. Label one envelope for each of these expenses, and each time you are paid from your employer or any other source, divide the money into each envelope so that you are accumulating the total amount due for each payment safely stored in the envelope. Remember, if you cannot pay the full amount of the bill, figure out what you can pay and contact your creditor.

EXAMPLE: The rent is $500 and is due the first of the month. Payday falls on the 14th and 28th of the month. Separate $250 out of your paycheck on each payday, and store it in the envelope marked Rent, either in cash or in a money order made out to the creditor who, in this case, is your landlord. Then, do the same for all of your other expenses that you have listed on your Cash Flow Statement and budget accordingly.

EXAMPLE #2: Insurance premiums will be less expensive when paid every six months or yearly so you will want to calculate the cost of the premium and divide it by the number of paychecks you will obtain during that length of time. Let's say your premium is $300 every six months and you can count on 12 paychecks

$$\frac{\$300}{12} = \$25$$

over that six-month period.

This means that you will need to set aside $25 out of each paycheck to pay that insurance premium every six months.

Calculate other household items such as groceries and miscellaneous expenses by saving those receipts for two or three months. Take an average of those months by adding all the receipts and dividing that Total by the number of months for which you have saved the receipts. This will give you a fairly accurate picture of the amount of money you need for those items.

When those months come around that are a little tighter than usual you can consider those miscellaneous expenses to tighten your belt and spend less money.

**Hint:** Whenever possible, purchase items in large packages. Why? The cost per pound and for each unit is reduced when the manufacturer does not have to spend as much on packaging their product.

My mother, God rest her soul had an extraordinary medical condition that threatened her life for most of my growing up years. When she was about sixteen years old, Mom accidentally drank an acidic solution that burned out the lining of her esophagus, and left her with scar tissue that would block the passage of food that she ate from following its' path down to her stomach to be digested. God had a purpose and plan for her life, and when I was in the sixth grade, He provided my mother with an equally extraordinary surgeon, Dr. Henry J. Heimlich, who had a practice in New Rochelle, New York. Periodically, my mother went back to New Rochelle for checkups. When I had graduated from high school, and we moved to Buffalo, New York, I was invited to join her on her next trip for a check up to see the city and meet the surgeon who was Gods' hands in adding 30 more years to her life! We Were Going to New York!! I had never seen the city and we were taking a plane ride and staying in a luxury hotel!! I was so excited! We arrived in the city, checked into the hotel, and took a train ride out to New Rochelle, a suburb of New York City. My mothers' surgeon was a wonderful person, so kind, gentle, and caring. After we met and her visit was over, Mom and I went to a charming little ice cream parlor for a treat, and when we returned to the city, we found a wonderful restaurant for dinner, and caught a movie at Radio City Music Hall, and watched the Rockettes!! This was a magical time for me, until the time came to return home.

My mother worked very hard to raise me and to make sure there was food on the table and a roof over our heads. However, there was never anything left over after those necessities were provided and the annual school pictures were bought, a practice Mom insisted upon. I have no idea whether Mom followed any systematic method for budgeting her money, but we found ourselves in Grand Central Station, trying to catch a train with no money. Mom and I put our heads together and tried to think of some way to solve this little problem, including calling the few friends we had acquired in Buffalo. None of our ideas produced a solution, and, although neither one of us said the words out loud, I'm sure we were both praying for help. God sent us an angel in the shape of an older man wearing a business suit, and when Mom approached this complete stranger and explained our predicament, he gave us the money for the train ticket back to Buffalo.

That trip to New York was resplendent with "first ever" experiences for me. I flew in a plane for the first time, stayed in a hotel, rode a train, and saw my mother out of control for the first time. The practice of budgeting resources including time, energy, and money requires taking the time to anticipate not only a basic foundation—in this case transportation down and back, but also taking the time to think and plan for the surprises that cannot be foreseen.

The foundation for everyday life naturally includes living expenses, but one must also recognize that entertainment and savings must also be included in a workable plan for those unexpected surprises—happy or otherwise!

# *MARCH*

## **MONEY ORDERS**

The second simplest method of managing your money is to convert that cash into money orders, especially for larger sums of money or for those bills that need to be mailed. Purchasing a money order when you are putting aside larger sums of money for monthly bills, such as the rent, will help you to resist the temptation to spend that money on other things that may seem like a necessity at the moment. A receipt comes with each money order, so make sure you indicate what bill was paid on your receipt before placing it in storage in the back pocket of that month's folder. Besides keeping track of your balance in your bank account booklet, this is the extent of the record-keeping for this method of management. This is a viable option for those people who enjoy immediate closure when spending money, but who still want the security of a financial institution behind payments made to creditors.

Money orders purchased at a bank or other type of financial institution can cost $2 or $3, but money orders can be purchased at some local post offices and most full-service grocery stores for less that $1 that are insured for $500 to $750. Take the time to shop around for the best value, and make sure the place of purchase is easily accessible so that you are not going out of your way to buy them.

The use of money orders epitomizes the simplicity that can be experienced by the individual who lives a life without the burdens of the materialistic world. Money orders used to pay the minimal amount of expenses such as rent, utilities, and insurance give immediate closure when each bill is paid. The user can enjoy a perfect credit rating because the individual is in complete control of the cash that is flowing from the bank account, and there will never be overdraft charges as a result of the check that should have been cashed weeks ago. The person who is recovering from financial mayhem, and who has suffered devastating loss as the result of divorce, bankruptcy, etc., can experience a sense of renewed self-worth, and self-control when exercising the discipline that comes from paying monthly bills on a monthly schedule, and learning to live a simple life within the budget that is allocated with each paycheck. The divorce rate in the United States remains stable at 50%, and as a result we may have become desensitized to the effects of this pain and misery both financially, and emotionally, as well as the painful effect divorce inflicts upon our community. I believe the reason God hates divorce is because of the pain and suffering that it inflicts upon His children. The simplicity of managing even one thing in our immediate lives successfully creates a realistic viewpoint about the rest of our lives, and that can lead us in a new direction that will nurture us back to perfect harmony within ourselves and our walk spiritually.

# *APRIL*

## THE CHECKING ACCOUNT............
### THE SIMPLEST CONTRACT

The checking account can be a reliable money management tool as long as you follow these basic rules:

1) Discipline yourself to record each deposit and check written <u>immediately</u>, including the date, the individual or company to whom the check was written, and the amount.

The quickest and easiest way to overdraw the account is to miss recording even one check. When sharing this account with someone else, this will seriously increase the number of "discussions" that occur over the checkbook. Did you know that financial difficulties are one of the primary reasons for divorce in our nation?

2) Make sure to record any charges withdrawn from your account by the bank such as monthly fees, additional fees for special services, and ATM withdrawal fees as they occur, in the record-keeping section of your checkbook, along with your record of the checks you write.

3) Never write a check unless the money is in the account to cover the entire amount. A check is only a promise that you make, assuring the person receiving the check that the money is available to pay the debt for the amount of money that is written on that piece of paper. Sometimes even the most reliable businesses and individuals can become victimized by circumstances beyond their control. Writing a check based on the promise made by your employer promising to pay you, may result in YOUR reputation being questioned.

The following story took place early in my marriage, before the children came along, and is about a contract "of the heart". I feel it is important to include these types of contracts in the discussion of money management, because a broken marriage contract not only affects the emotional and spiritual state of well-being, but it also affects the sense of security for the individuals and community. Choosing a life partner involves the rational decision process before allowing oneself to become emotionally or physically involved with that person. Word-of-mouth advertising applies to businesses as well as individuals, and as long as one is able and willing to hear the truth, loss can be avoided.

I am not a skeptic by nature. I have a tendency to believe what I am told, then question what was said to me much later. One of the fundamental "truths" I learned in my marriage, was that nothing could be accomplished, nothing useful or worthwhile could be valued by others unless "perfection" had been achieved by the giver, namely myself. One example of this frame of mind involves my love of cooking. I was not a professional chef, since I had never attended any formal classes from which I would receive a piece of paper saying that I knew what I was doing. One year I found an amazing recipe for fruitcake. No fruitcake jokes please! The process was slow, since the fruit had to ferment in rum for a long time before moving onto the next several steps required to put all the ingredients together for baking. The fruitcake was absolutely marvelous according to those who received them as Christmas gifts. The only person who did not receive the gift in the manner in which it was given—a gift from my heart—was the one it mattered most to me to be able to receive, namely my husband.

The Process of checking and balancing this "truth" helped me to realize the truth lies within myself on a fundamental level. I have no control over what anyone else thinks or feels except myself! I choose to believe that the things I create with my own hands are worthwhile gifts because God gave me the resources to create those things that are uniquely my own.

The process of checking and balancing the facts that are available will always serve to enable a person to make a rational decision based on the information that is available, whether it is for a checking account, a life partner, or funding for a college education.

# CONTRACTS

Contracts come in a variety of forms. Some contracts are easily identified as legal and binding, as when you sign your name on a legal document when taking out a loan, or agreeing to pay membership in a health club. Signing your name on the dotted line for the credit card (a revolving loan), the debit card, the check that promises that the amount written on that piece of paper will be paid to the payee, are all contracts that are legal and binding. As such, the agreement will be enforced by the law should your circumstances change in such a way that uphold-ing your end of the bargain becomes more difficult, or impossible to maintain.

Does this statement sound cold, harsh, or unloving? The truth is, if we lived in a perfect world, laws would never have had to be created, because everyone would live in a spirit of prosperity that would provide for everyone's needs. A spirit of prosperity is the attitude that there is plenty to go around. People who believe that this is the case, share freely with one another and do not expect to legally enforce the commitment made by the other party involved in the exchange. The contract provides security for the individual or business offering goods or services, and protects them from loss. By the same token, the written contract also protects the consumer by promising to honor the exchange in case of damage or any other problem with the merchandise or service provided by the dealer. This contract is provided in the form of a warranty, in which the manufacturer promises to repair or replace the faulty merchandise within a specified period of time after purchase. The warranty is included in the cost of the merchandise, so examine the warranty as carefully as the merchandise itself. Businesses that provide a service will, gener-ally, stand behind the work that has been performed, but it is always best to check with the Better Business Bureau, as well as with other people who have utilized that service. Word-of-mouth advertising is one of the most reliable tools for selecting a service provider.

The responsibility of entering into a contract ideally lies with both people involved in making the commitment, but realistically, the responsibility is yours to examine and objectively determine whether you are ready, willing, and capable of holding up your end of the bargain. The important issue is acknowledging whether the time is right for making such a promise BEFORE agreeing to the commitment. The Rational Decision Model can be used to help in the process of making the decision objectively, and while you are still free to say "No". Try to see yourself through the eyes of the person to whom you are making the commit-ment and ask yourself if you would accept a contract with that person. Here are a few questions to consider: "Am I truly free to take on this new responsibility?" Examine your income and liabilities objectively to determine the stress level of an additional responsibility. "Am I willing to leave this place and relocate some-where that will provide the resources to pay for my obligations?" This is an important question to consider when pondering a college degree funded by stu-dent loans, particularly if job placement will inevitably take you out of your present location. "Do my responsibilities to someone else make it difficult or impossible to fulfill an obligation to another?" This could include a spouse who is succeeding in your present location, or another person for whom you are responsible for another few years.

Examining alternative solutions as part of this decision making process will help you to decide whether this is the time to make a commitment. Rather than applying for those student loans, research other sources for financial support in the form of grants or scholarships. Perhaps it is possible to attend the health club without committing to a contract, or other clubs that do not require a commitment, but will allow spontaneous visits.

Contracts are an integral part of our society, providing financial and emotional security for all concerned. The financial commitment provides security for the business and individual, just as the commitment of two parties in a marriage provides security for the individuals involved, as well as for the community in which they live and work. Generally speaking, the longer the terms of the contract, the more Faith is involved in the commitment. For example, entering into a marriage contract requires that each person know that there is a mutual goal, and each partner will enhance the others' personal growth toward achieving that goal. Agreeing to pay back student loans is, likewise, based on the belief that the resources will be available to pay back the amount borrowed plus interest, when the time comes to repay the debt that will, ultimately, make it possible for others to borrow the money that will make their dreams come true.

The input of a trusted friend who can remain objective is invaluable when making these life-altering decisions. The smaller decisions such as spending habits may not require as much time and research, but still require a careful examination of the resources available in the shape of time, energy, and money.

A contract with God is quite a different experience than with another human being. A contract of the heart with God means that even when we are unable, or perhaps unwilling to fully participate in holding up our end of the agreement, God will always be faithful to us, for He said, "I will never leave you nor forsake you". How is this possible? All things are possible with God in control for He knows how this will all work out for us, and he can be patient and forgiving to allow us to separate from Him, and make our own decisions that will ultimately bring us back into the light of truth, that man will always let us down because we do not live in a perfect world, and the decisions we make for ourselves and for someone else will always be flawed as we respond to the imperfections we live with on a daily basis.

I was married and living in Buffalo, New York when I was pregnant with my son, Lyon. Lyon was born in the middle of March, so I was pregnant during the summer, fall, and early winter. I was working for the insurance company and the office was about a mile and a half from home, so during the beautiful seasons I was walking to work every day. When winter came with the first snowfall of the season, I decided to take the bus to work. Understand that during this period of my life I was not praying, for I had left my very new relationship with God behind me when I met and married my husband, and I was living life with no conscious communication with anyone except the human beings in my life. The snowfall was very wet and sloppy, and keeping my feet underneath me was not an easy task. I came to the street light and began to cross the street where the busses were admitting passengers. Several busses were on both sides of the street, and crossing put me in a position behind the bus I was planning to catch and in front of the bus from the other side of the street who, at that very moment was pulling up, sandwiching Lyon and I between the parked bus and the other who was moving on very sloppy, icy pavement. It was at that moment that I lost my footing and slid down into the gutter, about seven months pregnant, not light or agile at all! Before I knew what was happening, I felt two hands under my arms lift me up off the pavement, and set me down on the sidewalk to safety, as the bus in motion stopped inches from the bus I was planning to catch. As I turned around to thank the very strong man who picked me up and saved our lives, I saw no one there. No one was walking away, and no one was in sight!

Entering into a contract with God means that He will always be with us, He will always be waiting for us to return to Him for guidance, comfort, and direction. I believe that as a human being, I am the culmination of physical and spiritual reality, and as a spiritual being in a human body, I carry out the spiritual purpose that God intended for the community He chose for me in this life. I create the physical reality I live in by making informed decisions that let me know what is available to serve my needs, such as insurance, housing, banking, etc. but as I walk in His light of truth, God is in control of the outcome of those things that will ultimately fulfill His purpose for my life.

# *MAY*

## SHOPPING FOR THE CHECKING ACCOUNT THAT SUITS YOUR NEEDS

I will always encourage you to take the time to shop and compare, whether it is for a money order vendor, a checking account, or a major appliance. The reason there is more than one business offering a product is because each one wants your business and are offering what they feel is a better product than their competitor. This spirit of competition drives prices down and increases customer satisfaction. The same is true for checking accounts and I want you to understand the vocabulary and the hidden meanings in these labels. Here are some questions that you can ask that will provide the information you need to make a wise decision.

1) Does the institution provide free checking? If so, is there a minimum balance required to maintain the status of free checking?

Some financial institutions offer free checking to its' customers as an incentive to draw business and hence, increase their revenues. However, if you tap into that minimum balance that you are required to maintain to receive free checking, you could be charged a fee on your account until the minimum balance is re-established. Therefore, the account is not free at all! Here is why—If you must keep $400, for instance, in the account for one year, you are losing the amount of interest you could have earned by keeping that money in a savings account. There are some banks that do offer free checking without requiring a minimum balance. They are not very plentiful, so don't be surprised if you do not find one in your community.

2) Does the financial institution have a program in place that will cover any overdrafts by withdrawing that amount from your savings account or a Line of Credit, automatically?

Be careful! If you do qualify for a Line of Credit (which is much like a credit card account) or a similar fund, you are borrowing from the institution and being charged interest for that loan. Make sure you can pay off the balance each month to avoid interest charges that do not take long to build up.

15

3) Does the financial institution offer a Debit card that can be used to withdraw cash directly from your checking account without writing a check? Must you apply for the Debit card as you would apply for a Credit card or is it given automatically with establishment of the checking account? Less than perfect credit will mean denial of the Debit card, and if you are recovering emotionally from financial setbacks, this does not help.

Make sure that you record each Debit card withdrawal just as you would a regular check. Ask if there any extra charges associated with the Debit card that are over and above a regular checking account.

# <u>WRITING THE CHECK</u>

The written check is actually a standard contract you are agreeing to honor with the person to whom the check is written (Payee).

1) The top right hand side of the check contains the check number. Recording the check number in the RECORD portion of your checkbook is vitally important in keeping track of each check that is written, particularly when balancing the checkbook at the end of each month.

2) The next line is the date, indicating the date you are promising the money is in your account to cover the amount of the check.

3) The next line that is headed "Pay to the Order of", is the payee who will be submitting your check to the bank for fulfillment of the contract.

4) The next line_____$0.00, is the amount of the check written out in words on the blank line, and restated in numbers for positive verification of the amount of the check. Always write the words and follow with the change written in numbers/100, followed by a line to fill in the rest of the blank space. The entire space filled in will prevent anyone from filling in a different amount than what you are paying the business.

5) The left side of the bottom of the check can be used for a variety of purposes such as a note indicating what the check is being used for, or for any type of account number when paying bills.

6) Finally, and most importantly is your signature on the bottom right hand side of the check. No contract is complete without your signature, and the business and bank cannot accept the check without it!!

Some banks offer checks that have a carbon copy of the check under the original document. If this is the case, you may take the time at the end of the day to record your check in the record-keeping portion of your checkbook. However, if you do not have a carbon copy of each check, record the check (preferably at the counter), before closing your checkbook. When using a debit card, make sure to keep your receipt from the store in order to fill in the amount spent on which day to the name of the store, just as you would a hand-written check. This is a discipline that may not come as easily as with the hand-written document, but just as necessary.

# *JUNE*

## BALANCING THE CHECKBOOK

Each monthly section of this workbook contains a form to use with the following step-by-step instructions for reconciling your checking account each month. I have included a copy of this form for each month in case your financial institution does not have a form on the statement they send at the end of each period.

Please remember, the balance in your checkbook will usually not be the same as the bank statement, since you may have written checks just before the closing date of the checking account. That makes it necessary to reconcile your account with the statement sent to you monthly by the financial institution by using these simple steps:

1. Sort your checks numerically or by the dates they were written.

2. Subtract any of the service charges for new checks, overdraft charges, etc., that were not recorded previously from your checkbook balance.

3. Enter your new bank balance on Line 1 on the Right side of the Balance form. This is the amount of money you have left in your account according to the bank.

4. List the checks that you have written that are not included in the bank statement in the chart on the left side of the Balance form and enter the Total at the bottom of the chart. Subtract that total of those unpaid checks from the bank balance in Step 3 and write down the new balance on Line 2.

5. Add any new deposits that have not shown up on this statement and write them down on Line 3.

6. Now, calculate your final balance by adding the total amount of deposits that are not reflected in the statement (Step 5) to the new balance you found in Step 4. This amount should agree with your checkbook balance.

What in the world do Master Mix recipes have to do with balancing the checkbook? Not much, but I would much rather prepare the food than balance the checkbook! What are Master Mix recipes anyway? Think of these recipes as homemade Bisquick mixes. When you come home after a busy day and still want to make a nice dinner, preparing the Master Mix recipes beforehand just saves time and makes it a lot more economical financially, too. These recipes are designed to last for a month if you include the shortening. However, in light of recent studies that point out the risks involved in using the Crisco type shortening that is hydrogenated included in these recipes, I would recommend leaving out the shortening and using Canola oil instead when you are putting the recipe together to bake.

On the other hand, maybe there are some similarities between Master Mix recipes and balancing the checkbook! Balancing the checkbook prepares one for the next round of checks to be written, just as preparing the Master Mix in advance makes for an easier job preparing the meal. Also, both are acts of discipline for which the rewards come later, since the Master Mix recipes are designed to last for a month, as often as one balances the checkbook.

Delayed gratification that stems from self-discipline is a valuable lesson to learn. At the very least, it makes life just a little bit more fun when we anticipate owning something or doing something that we know we have to take the time to earn for ourselves. There is a sense of accomplishment that no one can give to us when we take the time to work through the process of achieving a goal we have determined for ourselves. Life has a way of taking unexpected twists and turns and as a disciplined person understands that although small rewards come periodically, the large rewards usually come much later.

I don't believe it's over till it's over, and I returned to school when I was 38 years of age. I wanted to have the credentials to legitimately pass on useful information that defined the person that I had become, and create the things l wanted to do with my life, a desire that I believe comes from God. I began to study in the field of Family and Consumer Science with an Extension option. The first year that I was in school, I was given the opportunity to work with our local county extension agent as an intern. The agent with whom I studied was also working with a woman who was acquiring her Masters Degree in a field associated with Geriatrics (the study of aging). The extension agent was assisting in the development of a seminar for caregivers who were working primarily with senior citizens. I was a Certified Personal Care Attendant at that time, and was asked to put together a presentation on the Personal Care Aspects of Home Care. The majority of people, especially women, have an unreasonable fear of public speaking, and this certainly did not exclude yours truly. I was taking the required Speech

Communication course required for my degree, as well as for the life of an educator, and did not feel that I had ever successfully given a group presentation.

Even as a Music Therapy major in Billings, I claimed my voice as my major instrument, and thus was required to take voice lessons. Of course, in order to receive a passing grade for my voice lessons, I had to perform in front of an entire class of music students, and my professor, bless his heart, defended my fear to the group of critical students who did not understand what a challenge the performance was for me. The music was all about me, and as I focused more upon myself, and not on the work I was doing, the more self-conscious I became. However, teaching the success I had achieved in the setting of people who were truly there to learn how to help someone else, naturally put all of us in a frame of mind that did not focus on our own performance level, but on the service we could perform for someone who would benefit greatly from our skill and knowledge. I organized the presentation, gathered all the equipment necessary, and gave the presentation to a group of about 65 People. The presentation was a tremendous success as was the entire seminar. The Extension agent approached me afterward and said, "Jan, you belong in education", which I then added to my degree.

This was one of the small rewards along the Path to achieving my degree. The degree itself took nine years to accomplish, since I did not want to take out government loans, and because my work and raising my children were so important to me that I chose to balance all three jobs as long as it took.

Life is a Process and enjoying the process is key to enjoying Life as it is given. ONE DAY AT A TIME!

## MASTER MIXES AND RECIPES

### BASIC MIX

8 cups all-purpose flour
1–1/2 cups nonfat dry milk
1/4 cup baking powder
1 tbs. salt
1–1/2 cups shortening

Cut shortening into stirred dry ingredients until texture of coarse crumbs. Store in an airtight container in cool place. For best *quality, use within one month.*
Yield: 10 cups

## WHOLE WHEAT MIX

4 cups whole wheat flour
4 cups white flour,
1/4 cup baking powder
2 tsp. Salt
1–1/2 cups shortening
1 cup nonfat dry milk
3–1/2 tbs. sugar

Cut shortening into well-mixed dry ingredients until the consistency of coarse crumbs. Store in airtight container in cool place. For best results use within one month.
Yield: 12 cups

## MASTER MIX RECIPES

## BISCUITS

3 cups mix
2/3 cups water

Combine mix and water and stir until blended. Knead on lightly floured surface 8–10 strokes. Roll out ½" thick and cut with biscuit cutter. Bake on ungreased baking sheet at 450 degrees F. for 10 minutes or until lightly browned. Yield: 8–10.

3 cups mix
2 tbs. sugar
1 egg, beaten
1 cup water

Add sugar to mix and stir. Combine egg with water to add to dry ingredients. Stir just enough to blend. Fill greased muffin tins 2/3 full and bake 20 minutes at 425 degrees F. Yield: 12 muffins

## COFFEE CAKE

3 cups mix
1/2 cup sugar
2/3 cup water
1 egg, beaten

Topping:
1/2 cup brown sugar
3 tbs. butter or margarine
1/2 tsp. cinnamon

Combine sugar with mix. Add water and egg and stir ingredients until moistened.
Combine topping ingredients and sprinkle over top. Bake at 400 degrees F. for 25 minutes in a greased 9x9" pan. Yield: 9 servings

## DUMPLINGS

1 egg, beaten
2 cups mix
1/2 cup water

Combine water and egg and stir into mix until blended. Drop by spoonfuls into bubbling liquid. Cook uncovered 10 minutes; cover tightly and steam 10 additional minutes. Yield: 4 servings

# JULY

The primary difference between a savings account and the credit card is that the savings account costs time, and the credit card costs money. Before we start examining the difference, I want you to understand the process of making a rational decision. So many times we may feel as though there are no choices in solving a problem, and there sits the credit card with a credit limit of $1000, $3000, or even $5000 that may seem like a perfect solution to at least a good portion of the problem. That is, until the bill that never seems to come to an end continues to arrive in the mail. In this portion of the workbook, we will discuss the Rational Decision Model that encourages the exploration of choices that will lead to a decision with the least amount of negative consequences.

## RATIONAL DECISION MODEL

A good decision is one based on enough information and insight so that the person making the decision will not regret it later.

1. Define the problem. Life is not usually isolated to one event that occurs all by itself at a time. Life is what happens while we are trying to make plans. Defining the problem means that you need to take the time to sort through everything that is going on in your life and figure out the REAL problem. Sometimes it helps to talk to a friend. Hearing yourself say the words and having someone else hear the words can be very revealing.

2. Determine several alternatives. Develop at least four possible solutions that could be used to solve the problem. Write down whatever comes to your mind, even if it sounds a little silly or crazy. It may not be so crazy after all!!

3. Gather information about the alternatives until the costs equal the benefits. Gathering information can mean shopping different businesses or talking to people—depending upon the type of problem you are solving.

It sometimes helps to have a friend to talk to, since two heads can be better than one. At any rate, make sure you explore each alternative you wrote down in Step Two, and think about them.

4. Weigh the costs and benefits about each alternative. Which alternative is going to cost the least amount of money, emotional strain, time, or effort? Look at all the alternatives and think about the long-term—not just today. Each one of us has our own level of tolerance. What may be completely stressful for one person may not be for someone else. Therefore, choosing the best alternative is really a personal choice, and that choice depends upon your own temperament along with the amount of support you are able to receive for the decision you have made.

5. Select the alternative with the most benefits over costs.

6. Act. Say the words, perform the deed, make the purchase—do whatever you need to do to complete this process and to have closure with this problem. Then, breathe a sigh of relief and give yourself a reward for a job well done.

7. Evaluate the actions. Life is a learning experience and since you came up with several solutions, now is the time to take a second look at those solutions and re-evaluate them. Would you have made a different choice now that you have the results of this first choice? How will you handle a similar situation differently when a problem arises again? Are you satisfied with the choice you have made or is there any portion of that decision that you would change?

The Rational Decision Model will serve you well anytime a difficult decision must be made, but for the purposes of this Money Management workbook, let us examine a financial scenario.

## LYON & EINSTEIN

My son Lyon has such a sensitive, nurturing spirit that his own family was not enough to satisfy his need for a parenting type of love in his life, even as a teenager. Lyon came home one day and asked how I would feel about having a dog in the house. We already had a cat, Ace, who had been a part of our family for ten years. Our home was Ace's territory, and he was not going to take kindly to someone else moving into his home. That was problem number one. Problem number two was, what else, money for food, visits to the veterinarian, and license so that dog would be legal. My priorities were in place, though, and the benefits of allowing Lyon his dog far outweighed the costs. We discussed these issues and I told Lyon that if he took a part-time job and used that money to feed the dog, pay for veterinarian visits, and buy the license, then I would allow him to have the dog. The business end of things covered, I let the idea go, thinking that this was just a hypothetical question that would never become a reality until…I came home one day and Lyon led me by the hand to my bed that was cradling the cutest little black ball of fur I had ever seen.

Lyon took complete charge of his new responsibility, which began with choosing the name "Einstein" for this highly intelligent animal we decided was a mix of Labrador, German Shepard, and Greyhound. Lyon spent all of his free waking hours training "Einie" to ask to go out to the bathroom, to sit, come, and stay. Lyon made all the appointments for the Veterinarian, and got a part-time job close to home to pay for the office visits and buy Einstein's food.

The temptation to decline Lyon's request for a pet of his own was strong, but the choice to nurture my son was more important than anything I could have done for him, as his mother. Lyon learned that he was trustworthy, responsible, and capable of creating a quality of life that was beautiful. Lyon also learned a little bit of what it feels like to be a parent who is totally responsible for another living creature, and a little bit of the rewards derived from the love and devotion that bonds the caregiver to the recipient. We always have the choice of focusing on all the negative's that life brings our way, but a fulfilling, joyful life requires that we take the risks that make us happy, and learn from those difficult times what strategies help us to cope, and then let those sad memories fade into the recesses unless there is more to learn from them.

Mary has found a beautiful television set with a 21" screen on sale for $600. She has an available balance on her credit card of $600, and the card carries an interest rate of 19%. Mary really wants to replace her 12" screen, even though it is only 2 years old.

Using the Rational Decision Model, let us determine if this would be a wise purchase for Mary.

1. The Problem
Mary's boyfriend likes to watch the ball games at Mary's place and is complaining about the small screen.

2. Determine the Alternatives

    a.   Does the store have a layaway plan, and what is the finance charge for the plan

    b.   Let Mary's boyfriend share in the cost of the new set

    c.   Use the credit limit on the credit card

    d.    Save the full amount of the cost of the set and pay cash in one lump sum herself.

    e.    Let boyfriend buy Mary's his own set and bring it to Mary's house or watch the games at his own place.

3. Gather information.

Let us examine each of these five alternatives:

A. The layaway plan. This will cost some time, but a lot less money than using her credit card.

B. Share the cost between them. This could cut the length of time in half, and would be an exercise for both Mary and her boyfriend in working together to achieve a goal.

C. Use the credit card. If Mary spends the limit on her credit card, the credit card company will charge interest that will put Mary over the credit limit. Then the company will charge her a monthly fee for as long as she is over the credit limit and may increase the rate of interest as well!

D. Pay cash in one lump sum. This will take some time, but there will be no finance charge, no additional charges on her credit card, and the set will be all her own!

E. What is the foundation of Mary's relationship with her boyfriend? Is Mary afraid that if he buys his own set and keeps it at home, she will never see him?

4. Which alternative would make you happiest? This decision depends upon your level of tolerance, patience, and your personal goals for yourself and the relationships in your life.

Before making a choice, read the following two short stories and the section on Credit Cards. You will then be able to make an informed decision about using the credit cards for Mary's purchase as well as your OWN!

Story #1

Purchasing a single item is infinitely simpler than planning an adventure. After all, it wouldn't be an adventure if every aspect of it COULD be planned.

Preparing for graduation, the internship, and a new life as a professional did not seem overwhelming until about two weeks before it was time to graduate. I sold the house and used part of the money to purchase a more reliable vehicle, and pay the housing costs on the house we would be living in during my internship. The internship was very intense and wonderful, leaving no room for the job search, but I planned a trip to another state where I was sure I would have no problem finding a job using my degree! That was my first problem! My second problem was my houseful of furniture that I had accumulated over the past twelve years, not to mention the things that could not be replaced such as a few choice textbooks, and papers I wrote that I could use professionally. Since I did not plan to return to Montana, I did not want to put all my belongings in storage here, so 1 rented a U-Haul truck, at great expense, drove cross country to Arizona, and set up housekeeping with my friends.

My daughter and I had been in touch with these dear friends for many years, and we even took a vacation to Arizona with them a couple years before this planned move. I really thought that was enough information to make a rational decision to move there. However, staying there with all my worldly possessions, seriously looking at the reality of jobs and housing, provided a much more accurate Profile than I had anticipated.

The process of making a rational decision requires a person take the time to develop at least four alternatives to solving a problem, and be willing to accept the truth, sometimes in spite of oneself.

However, identifying the problem can also mean that a Process is involved just to identify all the problems, for here is RARELY only one.

Selecting the most pressing problem and exploring as many solutions as possible, very often provides clarity and insight into the other problems, and solving the most pressing issue very often provides solutions to those other problems that are not the most urgent.

Developing a rational decision, by the very definition, means that one must set aside the emotional response to a situation in order to perceive the facts. Emotions set aside, one can look back and clearly understand the truth and, therefore, see what needs to be done to achieve some sense of satisfaction with the solution that was put into action. It is impossible to know if I would have seen the truth about the new home without taking all my possessions there with me, but in retrospect, I can say that if I had it to do all over again, I would have put all my belongings in storage and simply called our trip a vacation. I ended up selling all my furniture to a used furniture dealer in Arizona and storing all of.my books and household items in the friends storage unit until I could retrieve them a year later. Incidentally, I did stay in Montana, where this book was written, and my experience driving a (U-Haul truck across country gave me the opportunity to drive a friend down to her home in San Diego, since she had never done anything quite like this by herself before!

Acknowledging the positive aspects of the "adventure" helps to alleviate some of the pain of the losses we suffered (not just material). The importance of taking the time to rest in the company of good friends when considering those events that can be life changing, is absolutely key to one's success.

Food for Thought: As long as we learn something from a decision, especially those decisions that do not turn out as we planned, can we call that choice a mistake?

Story #2

## DYING FOR A CREDIT CARD

I was amazed at the offer I received in the mail for a credit card. I did not have a clue about the reality of using a credit card, but the timing was perfect. My little car really needed snow tires, and I knew that if I bought brand new tires, it would also extend the life of the tires I used for the rest of the year. I was only going to use the card for my vehicle, I promised myself.

You can probably guess that it did not take long to compromise my way out of that particular commitment, and not much longer for my "friends" at the Credit Card company to call me frequently because I had over-extended the limit on my card.

I have always considered myself to be a responsible person, and I support this statement by acknowledging that at this point in my life, I was a homeowner, a single parent providing for my two "Gifts from God", and a student working on a degree that would give something back to the world.

The phone calls from the Credit Card company made me question my self-esteem, and I had the distinct impression that I had to defend myself to a total stranger who could care less about all of my accomplishments, making me very angry.

I never wanted to take a second credit card to pay off the debt of the first card, as is so often the case. Doing so would have made my life far more complicated than I could handle with any degree of peace. Consequently, I had to make payment arrangements with the company that I could afford, and that would appease their appetites for my blood. Those arrangements did not stop the phone calls.

My children always knew when Mom finished another discussion with the Credit Card company by my reddish-purple complexion and the dazed look in my eyes. Observing Mom that upset and frustrated made my children, especially my daughter, equally frustrated and helpless. My daughter, Rose, came up with a brilliant solution to my predicament, and the company gave her the perfect opportunity to set the wheels of her solution in motion. The Credit Card company called one afternoon before I came home from work and school, and asked to speak to her Mom. Rose reported, ever so sadly that her Mom had died, and when the woman on the phone asked Rose what happened and when, Rose provided her with all the details of my demise. Imagine my surprise when Rose told me that the Credit Card company had called that afternoon and that she reported my death! I very nearly did have a heart attack! I must admit that I was tempted to stay six feet under, after thinking about her solution. Fortunately, I am honor bound to be an honest person, and did report that I was truly alive! I can't help but wonder what the people on the other end of the line must have been thinking! The chapters on Credit Card Management and the Rational Decision Model will provide some insight on the reality of credit card interest calculations. I provide feasible alternatives to making purchases without the accumulated interest of a revolving loan. The simple life without loans, and the peace attained in freedom from creditors, should be seriously considered when you explore the purchase of a credit card. Purchasing articles using a layaway plan is a secondary method you can use to establish a good credit rating, and taking a small loan from a bank or credit union for a vehicle or something of equal value, will also establish a positive credit rating, as long as you make your payments on time. Take on long-term debt to satisfy long-term goals, rather than for short-term goals, which can and do occur when only the minimum payment is paid on credit card loans. Patience, Prudence, and Perseverance are required when alternatives to credit card purchases are exercised. The immediate gratification of walking out of the store with your purchase in hand does not happen, but neither do the credit card bills that never seem to come to an end. The credit rating you establish now will stay with you for seven years after the debt is satisfied. Consider carefully before signing on the dotted line.

Each year, examine your credit rating in order to validate any errors that may be in place and to objectively evaluate your credit rating in order to apply for a loan. There are three companies who are responsible for the establishment of your credit rating and they are Experian, TransUnion, and Equifax. Their website is www.annualcreditreport.com. The toll free telephone number is 1–877–322–8228, and their mailing address is: Annual Credit Report Request Service, PO Box 105281, Atlanta, Georgia 30348–5281. Check your credit rating before applying for a loan, because each time you apply for a loan without knowing your credit rating, it s a mark against you, since it appears that your are looking for money. The credit score that is best is over 700, and least acceptable is less than 600, and this score may cost an additional fee to obtain.

# *AUGUST*

## CREDIT CARDS

Let us take a look at how the interest rate is calculated depending upon which card you purchase through one of your local banks, to really understand the implications of using the credit card for this and any other purchase.

There are three methods that credit card companies use to calculate interest rates to ensure their own profits. If you look at the fine print on the back of an application form at any bank in your community, you will see one of these three methods of Interest costs for consumer credit.

A. Previous Balance Method

The interest rate will be charged on the balance of the account before you make a payment.

Let us say you charged $200 on your credit card and made a $100 payment. The principle remaining is $100 and the monthly finance charge is 1.5%. The monthly finance charge is based on the monthly breakdown of an annual interest rate of 18% which is the interest rate indicated on the credit card application form. Calculate the monthly interest rate by dividing 12 (months) into the annual percentage rate indicated on the application. The bank will multiply the monthly finance charge times the original $200, which results in a finance charge of $3.00 for that month. That means that your finance charges will be 36% yearly as you continue to make new charges to this card. Dollar for dollar, 36 cents of each dollar will be applied to interest alone.

B. Average Daily Balance

Interest will be charged on the sum of the average owed during the month.

Now, suppose you charged $200 and made a $100 payment, leaving a balance of $100. In this case, the beginning balance of $200 is combined with the remaining principle of $100, which amounts to $300. Since the bill is only one month old, the balance owed is combined with the remaining principle and the two are averaged to $150. With the monthly finance charge of 1.5% times $150, you will be paying $2.25 in interest for that month. As you continue to charge on the card during the year, the end result will be an annual fee of 27%!!

C. Adjusted Balance Method

Now, let us say that you charged the same $200, paid $100 and had a remaining balance of $100.

The monthly finance rate of 1.5% will only be charged on the remaining balance of $100 or $1.50. Therefore, paying the balance of your charges each month will result in no finance charges at all!

Well, that explains why credit card companies advertise in the mail, magazines, and television, doesn't it!

Paying the balance of credit card charges each month will result in an excellent credit rating that will enable you to make larger purchases in years to come. However, this means that you must know how much money you can afford to spend that month and have the strength to stick with this reasonable amount of money as opposed to spending all the credit card company is offering.

Credit cards serve a useful purpose as long as you understand the long-term financial costs for wise management. When you do not use credit cards to add to your income by purchasing more on the credit card than you can afford to pay for in a month, the card can help you to establish a good credit rating. However, using the card to purchase an item that is too expensive to pay for in one month will continually accrue interest charges that can be overwhelming. When this happens, your good credit rating can be destroyed, making those long-term purchases such as a home, retirement, or college education for your children much more difficult to attain.

But, with wise management, a credit card can be used for vacations, since it is safer to carry than cash, for emergencies, sales, or to use instead of personal checks, since the credit card is more readily accepted. Also, check with your banker for credit cards that carry a significantly lower annual interest rate.

Let us return to Mary's dilemma with the boyfriend who wants the 21" screen television set. Mary came up with five possible solutions to solve her problem (or was it me?). She could explore the store's layaway plan, let her boyfriend share in the cost of the set, use the credit card limit on her credit card, save the full amount of the cost of the set and pay for it herself, or let her boyfriend buy his own set and bring it to Mary's house or watch the games at his own place.

I think it is easy to see that the credit card would be the most costly alternative financially. Remember, in this type of scenario, there are no "right" or "wrong" decisions—only a different set of consequences for each one. In the long run, you want to make the decision that you will not regret later on. Taking the time to examine all the choices and their consequences will help you avoid the pain of the consequences of a different decision.

## SOLUTION

5.6. Mary decided to put the set on layaway and her boyfriend will split the cost of the set with her. He was reliable and held up his end of the bargain. Now they both own the new set and are enjoying the larger screen at Mary's house. There won't be an issue with this decision unless they split up and have to deal with any purchases they made together.

7. Evaluate. What did Mary learn out of this experience?

She learned that her boyfriend is reliable and trustworthy.

Using the credit card is only one way of buying the things she wants.

Mary and her boyfriend do work well together in solving problems.

# *SEPTEMBER*

## <u>INSURANCE</u>

Let us talk briefly about insurance. Insurance plays an essential role in surviving in our world today. Without insurance to cover medical needs and emergencies, the quality of our lives can be seriously compromised.

We will talk about term and whole life insurance, but before we do that, I just want to impress on you that at the very least, you want to have the protection of health insurance for your body, and Liability insurance for your vehicle.

First let us look at health insurance. Health insurance will cover a large portion (usually 80%) of office visits for check-ups, hospital costs for emergencies including disability and surgery, as well as the medications involved in the treatment plan, physical therapy, etc. These medical costs can be greatly decreased, though, just by taking good care of yourself. Here are a few simple suggestions:

1) Eat a diet rich in nutrients with plenty of fruits, vegetables, whole grains, dairy, and proteins.

2) Get plenty of exercise; any time you can walk instead of driving to go to work or run errands, enjoy the fresh air and sunshine. Or, just go for a walk for the fun of it!

3) Giving up the habit of smoking, all by itself, will almost completely eliminate the possibility of developing lung cancer, emphysema, and a host of other lung diseases associated with nicotine. Cutting back on the amount of affianced soda pop and coffee, granulated sugar, alcohol, drugs and narcotics will also help you to avoid the onset of other health problems.

4) See your doctor yearly for a good check-up. If you do not have your own physician, check with your local hospitals and county medical society for low cost fitness check-ups. There are programs being developed all over the United States that provide affordable check-ups in order to promote preventive health care that will diagnose areas of concern before a serious situation occurs.

Once again, shop around for anything you need to purchase, including insurance. Ask your employer about health care insurance that is provided through a group insurance policy. A group policy costs less because the premiums, essentially, are paid by a large group of individuals rather than one individual. Besides that, the payments are automatically taken out of your paycheck, Easy!

Call several insurance agents and find out what other group insurance plans are available.

Also, check with Blue Cross/Blue Shield for individual insurance plans.

A Health Maintenance Organization (HMO) may be a viable alternative for you. I urge you to check out your local HMO's and gather information to use in making a sound decision. Remember that lesson from the Rational Decision Model?

The other type of insurance that is vitally important in our society is vehicle insurance, at the very least Liability insurance to cover any damage you cause to another vehicle or individual in that vehicle. A number of states require vehicle owners to carry liability insurance so that, if you cause an accident, the responsible party will pay the damages. Even if you are not legally required to carry Liability insurance, the peace of mind that comes with the knowledge that your responsibility for the accident will be covered can be priceless.

As with health insurance, though, an ounce of prevention is worth a pound of cure. Take it Easy! Don't drive when you are under the influence of emotions, drugs (prescription or otherwise) or alcohol.

Walk it off—Walk home—Stay where you are—Call a friend—Chill Out Man!

Always remember that your vehicle is also a weapon. Treat it with a great deal of respect. There are ALWAYS other vehicles on the road with you. You know the rules—make sure you axe thinking about them. In other words, avoid the accident before it happens.

# *OCTOBER*

## LIFE INSURANCE

I am not going into a great deal of detail about any one aspect of insurance. I want you to walk away, though, understanding what you need, and what you Do Not need to investigate for your own personal finance plan. That said, here is a foundation on Life Insurance.

The purpose of life insurance is to protect dependents from the premature loss of life of someone upon whom they rely for financial or personal resources. In other words, if you are responsible for another human being, whether they are your children or any other family member, blood relative or adopted, you will want to find a life insurance policy that will take care of them if you are not able.

There are two types of Life insurance—Term and Whole Life

Term insurance is pure insurance with no cash value. The cost of the premium (payment) is based on the likelihood of death. In other words, if Dad works in a dangerous occupation, the premiums will be higher than if he works in an office.

Whole life insurance is a combination of term insurance with the insurance company acting as an investment company. As premiums are paid into the policy, the cash value portion builds very slowly in the first years and then more rapidly later on. If you die, the policy pays your survivors the cash value and the difference between the cash value and the face of the policy.

So, if you are single and are not responsible to provide for anyone else but yourself, or if you are married and both of you are contributing to the household expenses, you really do not need life insurance. It is a personal choice that only you have the power to make for yourself.

### MY FAVORITE INSURANCE POLICY

I lived in Buffalo, New York during the time that my son was born. I was employed by an insurance company that provided every type of insurance protection that was availa6le to its' customers and employees alike. My favorite insurance policy, however, came in the shape of a four legged, green-eyed ball of fur named Jacob. Jacob had been a part of our little family for about three years before Lyon was born. Despite all the warnings from my co-workers about cats and newborns, we knew that Jacob posed no threat to our baby. Jacob was introduced to Lyon immediately upon Lyon's arrival to his new home, and a bond was formed between the two at that point in time. Jacob *was* right there whenever Lyon cried, just as attentive as Lyon's human parents. I did not really understand that Jacob had become our very own "guard cat" until, Lyon began to hold his head up independently, at which time I started to put him down on a blanket on the living room floor. Jacob would systematically situate himself on the corner of Lyon's blanket and posted sentry over "his Charge". Lyon and Jacob were in their designated positions on the floor, when a friend who had not seen Lyon for a little while decided to come up to our apartment for a visit. The sound of her footsteps on the stairs leading up to our apartment raised Jacob off Lyon's blanket, and when I opened the door to admit our company, Jacob started to attack our friend! I picked Jacob up very carefully, and introduced him to our old friend so that Jacob would let her into our apartment! This *became* the pattern in our home until Lyon began to walk on his own at eight months of age! I had to learn to "child-proof" the house in a hurry!

The cost of this insurance policy was minimal—a lot of love, a little food, and the money for veterinarian visits. The rewards abounded with the unconditional love that Jacob returned to those of us lucky enough to be a part of his pride for his lifetime.

# *NOVEMBER*

Guide to good eating: Every day eat different foods from each of the following food groups: Breads and Grains, Fruits and Vegetables, Dairy, and Fats.

Immediately upon my graduation from high school, my mother and I moved to Buffalo, New York. Our first apartment was located in the Italian section of town and our landlord taught me how to prepare a variety of her native dishes whose foundation is this Marinara sauce. I have always had a passion for cooking and one of the many advantages of cooking from scratch is the low cost of purchasing the individual ingredients compared to the cost of ready-made. The food is much more nutritious when made from my own fresh store of ingredients, and it is a gift of myself to anyone who partakes of the meal.

Jan's Marinara Sauce

4 (12-ounce cans tomato paste + 4 (12 ounce) cans water
1(14 ounce) can diced tomatoes
2—3 cloves garlic
1 small onion
2-TB. Olive oil
1 tsp. Oregano
1 large or 2 small bay leaves
1 tsp. Sweet Basil
I tsp. Marjoram
1/2 tsp. salt
1 TB. sugar
Red cooking wine or Worcestershire sauce
Parmesan/Romano grated cheese

Saute onions and garlic in olive oil. Add remaining ingredients and simmer approximately hours, stirring occasionally. Ideally, the sauce should be simmered with the lid off (if you don't mind cleaning the top of the stove constantly). The sugar cuts some of the acid, but for best results, prepare the sauce the day before you plan to serve it, and refrigerate overnight.

The following recipes are one's that I created while experimenting in my own kitchen for dinner.

## Ovenfried Chicken

1 whole cut-up chicken
1 cup all-purpose flour
1/4 tsp. salt
1/2 tsp. Pepper
1/2 tsp. Paprika
1/4 tsp. minced Garlic
1/2 tsp. dried Rosemary
1/2 tsp. Sweet basil

Preheat oven to 375 for chicken with skin on, or 350 for chicken without

the skin. Line cookie sheet with aluminum foil and spray evenly with cooking spray. Wash chicken thoroughly and dry in paper towels. Combine flour and seasonings, and dredge chicken in flour mixture. Place breaded chicken on prepared cookie skeet and bake 3o minutes, turn over and bake an additional 30 minutes.

Serve hot with Potato salad for a delicious summer meal.

## Turkey Enchiladas

1 pound ground turkey (or other favorite ground meat)

1 16 oz. Can refried beans
1 10 oz. Can green chile sauce
1 10 oz. Can enchilada sauce
8 burrito size tortillas
2 cups grated Monterey Jack cheese

Brown ground meat in skillet; add refried beans and green chili sauce and saute until bubbly. Heat tortillas in microwave oven in opened Plastic sack approximately 1 ½ to 2 minutes, or until soft and pliable. Pour half of the enchilada sauce in the bottom of a 9 x 12 inch cake pan. Spoon 1/4 cup ground meat mixture into each tortilla, fold all four sides to form a pouch, and place folded side down, into cake pan. After filling the pan, cover the enchiladas with the remainder of the enchilada sauce, and sprinkle the cheese over the top.

Cover with aluminum foil, and bake at 350 for 3o minutes. Toppings can include salsa, sour cream, olives.

Serve with your favorite salad, corn, or green beans.

I have written a number of articles based on Food and Nutrition, and this is one that gives a little insight into the process of enjoying life and accepting ourselves, as we are today, in the ever-changing process of growth. The facts presented about types of fats and their food sources may also be of value to increase your knowledge in maintaining a healthy balance in your food intake.

How many pounds did you gain after all the holiday festivities were over? We can use all the safe, familiar excuses like, "I didn't want to hurt her feelings," or "it looked so good, and I only get it once a year!"

The truth is, that a holiday celebration is not complete for any human being without food. The sense of celebration we hold in our spirit must be manifested to include the physical body as long as we live within this mortal coil, so why not embrace it, and deal with the consequences afterward? Besides, it gives us a new goal to work on, and that makes life interesting and challenging!

I only want you to exercise a little caution and prudence (along with diet and exercise in losing those unwanted pounds). Formal studies conducted by the Food and Drug administration talk about a healthy amount of fat in our diet that provides the necessary amounts of vitamins A, D, E, & K, at approximately 30% of our dietary intake. Just keep in mind, balance in all things.

This figure is based on the individual who is not trying to lose any weight. Certainly, you will want to eat less than 30% if you are trying to lose, but not less than 15–20% every day. Keep in mind that there are three types of fat that *we* eat that vary in their digestibility—that is how well the food can *use* the vitamins and discard the rest. The most digestible fats are found in monounsaturated fats of Canola and Olive oils. Research has shown that these oils actually reduce the risk of developing cancer cells.

Polyunsaturated fats, research has proven, yields the highest percentage of cancer-causing properties. Polyunsaturated fats found in corn, safflower, sunflower, and soybean oils appear to digest the quickest, leaving the smallest amount of residual fats in the bloodstream, also leaving the smallest amount of protection against cells running amuck.

Saturated fats found in dairy products, red meat, palm and coconut oils, is the most difficult fat for our bodies to digest and, therefore, lingers in our bodies to wind up being stored! This can lead to heart disease, and many visits to the doctor's office!

Losing weight and improving one's health is really a matter of improving the balance of exercise, fiber from fruits, vegetables and grains, fats to keep your eyes and skin healthy (Vitamins A & E), your bones strong (Vitamin D& C), your blood healthy enough to coagulate when bleeding occurs (Vitamin K), and water to flush out toxins. Once you start moving, replacing those Sticky buns with salads and fruits, and shedding those extra pounds, you will wonder why it was so tough to get motivated to feel so much better!

Enjoy the process, because life is a process of growing and changing! These changes provides us with the opportunity to learn something new about ourselves and gain a new perspective on the world in which we live, which is ALWAYS changing!

# GOAL DEVELOPMENT EXERCISE

Savings are the most effective method for rewarding yourself for all the hard work that you perform at your job. The savings that you set aside out of each paycheck helps you to realize that you are not just working for everyone that you are obliged to pay in order to keep a roof over your head and food on the table. The accumulation of ANY amount of money, wisely spent on some article that helps you enjoy life and derive a sense of accomplishment is vital to living a rich, rewarding life. Let us decide what to save for!

This Goal Development Exercise that I will describe came out of the internship I practiced while obtaining my degree in Family and Consumer Science Education. The Purpose of the exercise was to help students in the midst of transition take a step back and objectively examine their heart's desire for their lives, by writing down and discussing their goals with other members of the group. The group feedback is very helpful in gathering information that will lead to the accomplishment of the goals.

The exercise is most effective when practiced by a group of people who will be working together to accomplish the goal. The exercise is also highly effective when practiced by a group of people who have a common frame of mind, such as being in transition together. Each person will need several sheets of paper and a pencil. Designate one person as the leader who will facilitate the discussion after each portion of the exercise is completed.

## STEP I

Before writing anything, each person needs to bring to mind those things that will give him or her a sense of joy, accomplishment, and satisfaction when that task is performed. This task can be anything from a particular career goal, owning a home, having children, or obtaining an education. The important thing is to make those goals outwardly visible, because those types of goals are easily measured. The intrinsic goal, such as happiness or maturity, will happen with the accomplishment of the outward and visible goals. For the next eight minutes, each person in the group needs to write down those goals that they would like to have achieved in the next five years—as many as each person can bring to mind.

Each member may now examine their own list and find three separate categories within that list. One such category may be buying a new home, or pursuing a career goal, or planning the vacation. Discussion can begin at this point when help is needed to discover these categories. Now that these goals have been identified, each member needs to decide which goal requires the most immediate attention. This can be based upon which goal will take the longest to achieve, or the one that will be the easiest to begin processing. Group discussions at this point will help each member of the group develop an understanding of everyone's hopes and dreams, but will also help each person to receive clarity, and a reality check for the achievement of the life goal. The first goal that you have decided upon is the Long-Range Goal.

## STEP 2

Step 2 helps each person to define those things that will need to be in place in order to achieve the Long-Term Goal. For example, in order to practice in a particular field, perhaps a level of education is required. The purchase of a home requires a down payment as well as finances to cover closing costs and insurance. The next eight minutes are spent writing down those things that must be in place, and the discussion this time will focus on what, specifically, needs to be accomplished, as well as the methods to achieve those goals. This goal is defined as the Mid-Range Goal.

## STEP 3

This step deals with the question "What can I do today to begin the process of achieving my goal?" A college degree requires funding, and money can be found from grants, scholarships, and loans. This information takes time and energy to gather, but making the first step of visiting your local campus is something you can do today. Purchasing a home also requires funding, but what type of home do you want? Many styles are available to choose from such as modular homes, log homes, condominiums, just to name a few. There are a variety of financial packages available that may include the purchase of land along with the home, rent-to-own, and lease options. These are questions that can be answered today that will set a path to help you achieve your long-term goal. This goal is defined as the Short-Term goal.

These goals are not set in stone, and priorities need to be examined whenever life altering events occur, or approximately every five years. I am going to interject some words of truth that are meant to be used as a source of encouragement, no matter what type of goal you are attempting to achieve. There is nothing easy about change, but change is a natural part of our lives. There was change in our family structure when we were born, when we left the nest, when we married or divorced, and each step along the way to old age. These changes come about so naturally that we hardly seem to notice because we expect them, and they are part of our comfort zone. The changes we are talking about with the Goal Development Exercise may very well take us outside of our comfort zone, where we are testing the waters of something that we never thought could happen for us. We do not need anyone to tell us that we are reaching far beyond what we "should" be doing because we tell it to ourselves. I cannot stress enough how important it is at this point of your journey to find people who have reached such a goal to be a new community that will give you the encouragement that you need, and who will help you to see that your goal is not beyond your capabilities and intelligence. Finding a new direction in life can be scary, but remember that the goal here is not to give up on the dream, but to give up the fear. Change on the inside, a change of heart, does take longer than the change on the outside, our physical environment, but without first experiencing a change of heart, the outward visible signs of that change will mean nothing and will not last. So, decide what it is that you want, gather the information that you need to begin this new life, and hold it up in prayer for guidance and revelation. Pray for a change of heart as you work toward your goals and trust that your Higher Power will be faithful to provide everything that you need.

Gathering information that is needed to accomplish each goal can have the potential of developing a joy and satisfaction in knowing that one can exercise a degree of control in one's life. This joy comes as one recognizes that wealth is not just measured financially, but by the freedom that comes from exercising choices for one's life.

# DECEMBER

## SAVINGS PLANS

Please excuse the old saying "Time is Money" and "A penny saved is a penny earned" but they are just as true today as they were before our society was overwhelmed by the idea of Instant Gratification that seems to be so important to some people in our culture.

Delayed gratification (waiting for the reward) brings about a multitude of rewards such as the development of patience with ourselves, and those with whom we develop relationships. It enables us to work toward a goal until it is achieved—a quality that develops perseverance that is essential to success in a number of life endeavors. It also can save a lot of money as we have just discovered in the section on credit card management.

Please notice on the Liabilities side of each monthly Cash Flow Statement, that I have listed Savings first. This is because I think it is vitally important to pay yourself, hopefully first, when you are working hard just to make ends meet. Developing the habit of saving is truly less about the actual cash than it is about discipline and self-sacrifice. The most effective way to develop the habit of saving is to establish a goal-that is, decide what you want to purchase that will not take very long to accomplish. The goal does not have to be enormous, as long as you want it enough to make it happen and know that you will have a sense of accomplishment when you have achieved the goal. Developing this discipline in your life will save you the cost of interest rates charged on credit cards and loan payments, and will develop a level of self-esteem and self-control that comes with discipline and stick-to-it-ness!!

The level of your income will best determine the type of savings that best suits your needs in the beginning. Ideally, taking out 10% of your income before you spend your money on anything else is an effective way to save. But, if that is not possible, let us begin with coins in a jar. You will be amazed at how quickly a little "nest egg" will grow by placing any manner of coins in a jar each time a family member deposits spare change. By the way, if the entire family is contributing, the entire family should have a conference to decide what the goal will be. Count the amount of change accumulated at the end of the first month, write it down on your Cash Flow Statement, and continue to save at least this amount each month. How long will it take to achieve your goal? Answering this question will be a source of encouragement for everyone to make it worthwhile to maintain the discipline.

Establishing a habit of saving for small items, and giving yourself little rewards out of those savings will enable you to save for the more long-range goals that will cover emergencies, education, retirement, and buying a home.

First, let us examine the emergency fund. The car quits and needs costly repairs. Someone has an accident and your insurance has a $500 deductible 'or you have no insurance at all! Three months salary is a good amount of money to have set aside for such emergencies. Bear in mind that this also should be established as a goal. However, the sooner you complete this goal, the better!

Think about this—The television set is getting old and you know you will need to replace it soon. There is a lovely set at your favorite store that is selling for $500. Eight months later you have set aside $800 by making some sacrifices and putting aside $100 toward this goal each month. After you have accumulated the first $200, open a savings account and continue to add $100 each month. You are now earning interest on your savings! Surprise! Your television set is on sale now for $349.99 and you have saved $450 toward your emergency fund.

The money you have saved in the bank is called a Liquid Asset. This means that you can draw it out whenever you need it and there will be no charges enforced by the financial institution for withdrawing funds before a designated period of time has passed. The emergency fund and the savings for those short-term goals, like a vacation or small appliances for the home, are best kept in a savings account that you can draw upon when you need it. However, the long term goals such as the children's education, purchasing a home, or planning for your retirement need to be kept in a fund that you cannot draw upon so easily.

One of the reasons it is important to establish a working relationship with a financial institution is that you will be able to have access to a bank officer who can run what is called an AMORTIZATION SCHEDULE that will give you an idea of how much you will need to save in order to plan for those long term goals I mentioned. An Amortization schedule is now on a handy-dandy computer program at your financial institution. The schedule takes into consideration the length of time you have to save toward the goal, the amount of money you wish to spend, and the future value of that money in the number of years you need to calculate. Future value is the estimated value of the dollar based on the antici-pated 3% inflation rate that we have lived with for a very long time.

Now that you know how much money you need to save, let's talk about some simple savings plans that will help you on your way. Series EE **Savings Bonds** are an excellent way to put aside money, and are easily purchased at most banks for $25. That $25 will purchase a $50 bond that will continue to earn interest for 30 years. Hold on to that bond for at least five years, since bonds increase in value each month. Cashing the bond before five years will cost you three months inter-est and remember, that interest is being paid on $50. Purchase bonds as often as you can, and leave them as long as you can to earn the maximum amount of money possible. Officers at your financial institution will be able to share more savings plans than I wish to cover in this workbook. I encourage you to visit with them about other options that will fit into your budget and lifestyle.

While you are investigating savings plans, I would also encourage you to visit with a broker at one of your local investment firms. Ask them about the rates on **Mutual bonds.** Mutual bonds take the money of many investors and buy and sell large blocks of stocks. This makes investments in mutual funds much safer than investing in a single company alone. Some mutual funds can be purchased for as little as $50.

# TITHING

Mutual Funds, Savings Bonds, and Certificates of Deposits (CD's), are all fine investment plans that will yield a financial return. The most important invest-ment you can make as a Christian, that will guarantee returns over and above anything you can imagine, is your investment of at least 10% of your time, energy, love, or cash into God's storehouse. Share out of your abundance, and with joy, for it cannot be pleasing to God if there is not joy in the giving.

Tithing is an investment in your relationship with God that is built upon a foundation of Trust, Faith, and Love. God knows your wants, needs, and desires before you even ask, and nothing pleases Him more than being invited daily in your walk that will fulfill all of those wants, needs, and desires. Tithing completes the circle of generosity that began with God in Heaven, and is linked to his chil-dren through His son and the Holy Spirit. Withholding our offering stops the cycle, because it stops the flow of Love the Father has for His children, just as a dam stops the flow of water in a stream. Money is the easiest commodity to part with because it requires no relational sharing, but when that is not possible, money is acceptable.

The truth is that money is a commodity that can enhance the quality of our lives when managed in such a way that we are earning an equal amount in our investments as we earn from our employment. This is the very definition of financial success. But, as surely as money comes, it can surely be taken from us. A savings plan can certainly cushion the fall, but in the end, our ability to deal with life's circumstances inevitably boils down to our own level of self-esteem that determines how well we deal with financial pitfalls. Why? If you value your own self-worth with regard to the amount of financial security you possess in your life, you may feel so ashamed, remorseful, frightened, or full of despair when a crisis occurs, that you may be unable to discuss your situation objectively with your creditors, and that, dear reader, is the purpose of this workbook. I want you to be able to discipline yourselves before one of those difficult circumstances occurs in your life so that you will not be left without any financial support or tools to recover from the crisis. As you learned from the section on credit card management, there are no "quick fixes" and anyone who is trying to sell you one already has taken care of their own needs.

One of life's most stimulating challenges is that of developing an awareness of our "self". In order to better understand who we are and how we change and grow is to learn how to develop strategies for dealing with, and overcoming the circumstances in our world that affects our lives.

I can only hope that this workbook has given you some of those tools.

Sincerely yours

# *BIBLIOGRAPHY*

1. New York State College of Human Ecology
    Cornell University, Ithaca, New York
        Professor Ramona K.Z. Heck

2. <u>Economic Issues for Consumers</u> 5th Edition
    Roger LeRoy Miller
        West Publishing Co., St. Paul, New York, Los Angeles,
    San Francisco
    Copyright, 1987

3. Dr. Deborah Haynes
    Montana State University, Bozeman, Montana

4. Michigan State University Extension Publications

5. Advance By Choice Program, Montana State University, Bozeman, MT